W9-AZD-598

Garech Browne collection of Claddagh rings

Photograph courtesy of the National Museum of Ireland

THE STORY OF THE CLADDAGH RING

Published in 1997 by Mercier Press
PO Box 5 5 French Church Street Cork
Tel: (021) 275040; Fax: (021) 274969
e.mail: books@mercier.ie
16 Hume Street Dublin 2
Tel: (01) 661 5299; Fax: (01) 661 8583
e.mail: books@marino.ie

Trade enquiries to CMD Distribution
55A Spruce Avenue
Stillorgan Industrial Park
Blackrock County Dublin
Tel: (01) 294 2556; Fax: (01) 294 2564

© Sean McMahon 1997

ISBN 1 85635 189 0
10 9 8 7 6 5 4 3 2

A CIP record for this title is available
from the British Library

Printed in Ireland by ColourBooks Ltd
Baldoyle Industrial Estate Dublin 13

Published in the US and Canada by
the Irish American Book Company,
6309 Monarch Park Place, Niwot,
Colorado, 80503
Tel: (303) 530-1352, (800) 452-7115
Fax: (303) 530-4488, (800) 401-9705

This book is sold subject to the
condition that it shall not, by way of
trade or otherwise, be lent, resold,
hired out or otherwise circulated
without the publisher's prior consent
in any form of binding or cover other
than that in which it is published and
without a similar condition including
this condition being imposed on the
subsequent purchaser.

No part of this publication may be
reproduced or transmitted in any
form or by any means, electronic or
mechanical, including photocopying,
recording or any information or
retrieval system, without the prior
permission of the publisher in writing.

THE STORY OF THE CLADDAGH RING

SEAN MCMAHON

MERCIER PRESS

IRISH AMERICAN BOOK COMPANY (IABC)
Boulder, Colorado

If you had known the virtue of the ring,
Or half her worthiness that gave the ring,
On your own honour to contain the ring,
You would not then have parted with the ring...

The Merchant of Venice, V. i. 216-9

CONTENTS

ACKNOWLEDGEMENTS

Thanks are due to Clodagh Doyle of the National Museum and Críostóir Mag Fhearaigh of the Central Library, Derry.

THE OLD CLADDAGH RING

The old Claddagh ring, sure it was my grand-
    mother's,
She wore it a lifetime and gave it to me;
All through the long years, she wore it so proudly,
It was made where the Claddagh rolls down to the
    sea.
What tales it could tell of trials and hardships,
And of grand happy days when the whole world
    could sing –
So away with your sorrow, it will bring love to-
    morrow,
Everyone loves it, the old Claddagh ring.

With the crown and the crest to remind me of
    honour
And clasping the heart that God's blessing would
    bring,
The circle of gold always kept us contented,
'Twas true love entwined in the old Claddagh ring.
As she knelt at her prayers and thought of her dear
    ones,
Her soft, gentle smile would charm a king;
And on her worn hand as she told me the story,
You could see the bright glint of the old Claddagh
    ring.

It was her gift to me and it made me so happy,
With this on my finger my heart it would sing;
No king on his throne could be half so happy
As I am when I'm wearing my old Claddagh ring.
When the angels above call me up to heaven
In the heart of the Claddagh their voices will sing
Saying, 'Away with your sorrow, you'll be with us
    tomorrow,
Be sure and bring with you the old Claddagh ring.'

Patrick B. Kelly

INTRODUCTION

It has a distinctive design – one of the best known in the western world: two hands holding a crowned heart. Its motto is unexceptionable: 'Let love and friendship reign' and its origins, its true origins, are shrouded in mystery. The Claddagh ring is old – at least 200 years – but no one is quite sure how it originated, where the distinctive design came from and why it became associated with the most famous fishing village in Ireland. This book tries to separate the fact from the fantasy, not decrying the myth but seeking to discover from history and tradition something of the story of a peculiarly Irish love-token. Our search will take us to Galway, of course, and Iar-Chonnacht but we will also look at the tradition of token rings worldwide and go back as far as the the Sumerian civilisation of the fourth millennium BC.

Our starting place is Galway, that city of the western seaboard, which has had such a colourful history. It began as a Norman fortress and then when the de Burgos became Burkes and more Irish than the natives in the thirteenth century, it passed into the hands of a number of mercantile families who ruled it as an independent city-state. The remoteness of the town and its lack of accessibility except by sea allowed them to make it a rich Anglo-Irish city, independent of its Gaelic hinterland and, because loyal to the Crown, untroubled by the attentions of English viceroys in Dublin Castle. For three centuries it enjoyed a golden age as a busy seaport and centre of trade with the continent. Its tendency to take the wrong side in England's wars led to its despoliation at the hands of Cromwell's armies in 1652, and forty years later it was occupied by Williamite forces. The final blow came a century and a half later when the great Famine of the 1840s seemed to take the heart out of it.

In the years that followed, its recovery was real but agonisingly slow. It was about this time that the first Claddagh rings appeared in substantial numbers, the city's jewellers having discovered that the design of the ring had become very popular, having been named after the fishing village that was situated at the edge of town on the *cladach* or foreshore of the beautiful Galway Bay. The history of this independent village beside, yet unattached to, an independent town is a fascinating one and the saga of the ring and its design is even more fascinating but perplexing as well. What part did Margaret of the Bridges, the daughter of John Joyce and widow of Don Domingo de Rona, play in its origin, and how was the slave of the goldsmith from Algiers involved? The tale is complicated, intriguing and mysterious and, as so often, one is left with conjecture and the feeling that 'no one knows for sure'.

Galway is now a lively, exciting and prosperous city. Its modern efficiency blends well with its air of historical importance and it is a model of how past and present, Irish and Anglo-Irish, culture and industry, scholarship and technology, may be combined in one vibrant living space. The Claddagh ring is appropriately on sale in many of its shops and it is but one of several symbols of a town's capacity for resurrection.

1

GALWAY – 'CITIE OF THE TRIBES'

The city of Galway, the principal town of Connacht and the administrative centre of the county, lies on the mouth of the short Galway river, on the northeast shore of Galway Bay, the beautiful inlet that separates County Galway from County Clare. It is, in the words of the poet Mary Devenport O'Neill (1879–1967), 'a town tormented by the sea' and even the casual visitor cannot but be aware of the bay before and the long stretch of Lough Corrib behind. It came into existence as a settlement between the years 1232 and 1243, when Richard de Burgo and his fellow Anglo-Normans wrested the land from territory belonging to O'Flahertys and O'Hallorans and built a redoubt and castle. The area had already had a fortification, known as *Dún Bun na Gaillimhe*, its purpose to defend the ford at the Corrib, and it was inevitably the scene of recurring contention between the rulers of Connacht and Munster. According to the *Annals of the Four Masters* (1599) it was built 'by the Connachtmen' in 1124, and in 1132 Conor, King of Munster, dispatched a force under Cormac Mac Carthaigh, who invaded by sea and took the fort. They record further incursions in 1149 and note that a Hugh O'Flaherty held the fort successfully against de Burgo in 1230.

The *Annals* characteristically include the traditional legendary account of the source of its name. The place, the scribes record, takes its title from the river called *Gaillimh* which was the name of the daughter of a local king Breasal, a chieftain so pre-Celtic as to be mythic, who drowned in its waters. A famous map of Galway dated 1651 marks the rock where the fatal accident occurred. It was the same father who gave his name to Hy Brasail (*Í Breasail*, Breasal's Isle), the lost city of Atlantis. As Gerald Griffin put it:

Men thought it a region of sunshine and rest,
And they called it Hy-Brasail, the isle of the blest.

The seventeenth-century writer Sir James Ware, writing in Latin, is not entirely convinced about this: '*Flumen Galviam, urbem nomini suo adoptasse videtur, sed nominis rationem venentur alii.*' ('The river seems to have given the city its own name, Galway, but others may find a different source for its title.') The most scholarly of the early historians of the city, James Hardiman (1782–1855), suggested with more logic, but not more accuracy, in his monumental *History of the Town and County of Galway* (1820) that the name might have something to do with the Irish word *Gall* (a word applied to Gauls, Normans, Anglo-Normans and Englishmen as history and invasion decreed). He suggested the town may have been called Ballinagall which he renders as Foreignerstown. *Gaillimh*

is a word that remains obstinately difficult for linguistic topographers to construe.

By 1396 the town had become a royal borough, the letters patent being issued by Roger Mortimer, Earl of March, the lord lieutenant of Richard II of England (1367–1400). The move was political and well bethought since the local de Burgos, now headed by Mac William *Uachtair*, had become, in the words the seventeenth-century historian, Archdeacon John Lynch (himself sometime headmaster of Galway Free School), used to describe them in his book *Cambrensis Aversus* (1662) '*Hibernicis ipsis hiberniores*' ('more Irish than the Irish'). Though set in undentable Gaelic Connacht, Galway became an island of English speech and culture and the main stronghold of the Crown's power in the west of Ireland.

Its isolation from other centres of Anglo-Norman or English concentration such as Kilkenny or Carrickfergus at a period when land journeys across Ireland were tedious and dangerous meant that the power exercised by the Crown was often slight. It was a long way from Dublin Castle in every sense. The town's access to the sea and the resultant growth of trade with Spain, the Netherlands, France and the Baltic seaports increased its prosperity and independence. It also gave it a special atmosphere, a sense of internationalism which was in notable contrast to the insularity and provincialism of most other Irish towns. From early times the quays and the waterfront inns were full of foreign seamen. Galway was different, and a self-consciousness of its commercial independence increased its political autonomy. It was a kind of city-state virtually ruled by the magnates who had gained authority with riches, with chief power invested in its mayor, an office formally established in 1484 by letters patent from Richard III's lord lieutenant.

The best known of these ruling families were called the 'tribes', the name given by Cromwell's soldiers in 1652. They were of English or Anglo-Norman descent, fourteen clans in all (in alphabetical order): Athy, Blake, Bodkin, Browne, Darcy, Deane, Font, French, Joyce, Kirwan, Lynch, Martin, Morris and Skerrett. Of these the premier tribe were the Lynches, who supplied the first mayor of the city in 1484 and eighty-three others between 1485 and 1654. It was Mayor Dominick Lynch who founded the excellent Free School in 1580 and the family has left one of Galway's finest architectural relics, Lynch's Castle, at the junction of Shop Street and Littlegate. It may also have added a lurid word to the English language. James Fitzstephen Lynch, who was mayor in 1493, is believed, as the presiding judge, to have had to sentence his own son to death for murder. So great was his respect for the law that he faced down riots organised by his own family and carried out the sentence himself. The story may be just that but it is said to have given the term 'lynch' to the peremptory hanging of a prisoner. (Some Americans, it must be said, claim a certain Colonel Lynch (1742–1840) of Virginia as the source.)

The members of the different 'tribes' naturally showed differences of personality and character – the Blakes were 'forceful' and the Joyces, the tribe most closely associated with the story of the Claddagh ring, were known as 'merry' – but all showed unswerving loyalty to the English Crown and the Catholic Church, the latter allegiance causing them considerable trouble after the English Reformation. The epithets traditionally associated with these ruling families are given in full in *A Statistical and Agricultural Survey of the County of Galway* made by Hely Dutton in 1824: Athy – suspicious; Blake – positive; Bodkin – dangerous; Brown – brave; Dean – devout; Darcy – stout; French – prating; Joyce – merry; Kirwan – stingy; Lynch - proud; Morris – plausible; Martin – litigious; and Skerrett – obstinate. (Some of these descriptions seem to be suggested by the names – 'dangerous' Bodkins and 'devout' Deans – and the others may be the result of vernacular history.) Under their care the city prospered and cultural and mercantile links with the continent strengthened. The medieval city was severely damaged by fire in 1473 but out of its ashes rose a well laid-out township which by the seventeenth century boasted many fine houses, some showing perhaps Hispano-Moorish details with towers, archways and walled courtyards. The famous Spanish Arch down by the Claddagh Quay is a relic of this period of prosperity.

The town could not help but be aware of its isolation from its hinterland, set as it was in fairly unruly territory. For centuries the Gaelic way of life persisted among the inhabitants of the Connacht territories that surrounded the loyal city. Like Ulster, where the old order lasted until the beginning of the seventeenth century, the way of life – hierarchical, pastoral, manorial and martial – could hardly have been more different from the urban closeness and market-place orientation of the pocket city. It was, thanks to Norman influence, easy to fortify, and succeeding city fathers had reason to keep the defences in good order for fear of incursions from the local clans. A Corporation edict of 1518 forbade any inhabitant to receive into his house, 'at Christmas, Easter, nor feast else, any of the Burkes [as the de Burgos now called themselves], MacWilliams, Kellys, nor any sept else without licence of the Mayor and council, on pain to forfeit £5, that neither O nor Mac shall strut nor swagger through the streets of Galway.' The word 'ferocious' which they used to describe the likely enemy, the O'Flahertys, was not entirely unjust. The burghers of Galway could not help looking over their shoulders and tended to use the seaway for exits and entrances, rather than risk crossing the hostile territories.

Yet even inside the town's purlieu was a tiny piece of a much older civilisation. It was a fishing village built along the flat stony northern shore of the bay. It took its name from its topographical situation: Claddagh, from the Irish word, *cladach*. In the story of the ring that bears its name it is the part of the town that will concern us most.

The English break with Rome did not at first affect Galway's prosperity. Its virtual autonomy continued and its rule by the oligarchy of merchants kept its character. The edict of Henry VIII in 1536 forbidding any 'Irish usages and customs' in the city did not much dismay the essentially non-Gaelic inhabitants and its loyalty to the English crown was still unquestioned. Elizabeth I confirmed the town's charter in 1579 and appointed the mayor as 'Admiral of Galway bay and the Aran islands' (though the fishermen of the Claddagh had other ideas). When in 1594, during the Nine Years' War, Red Hugh O'Donnell appeared on its outskirts demanding supplies, he was refused, and though he burned some houses on the fringe of the settlement he made no attempt to take the town.

Living in the town at the time of this visitation were Oliver Óg Ffrench and his wife Margaret, whose first husband had been a Spanish wine merchant of La Coruña. She became famous as *Maighréad na nDroichead* because of her having commissioned and paid for 'severall stone bridges through all Connaught from Galway to Sligoe' as Roderick O'Flaherty (1629–1718) wrote in about 1684 in his topographical history of the region. (The work was edited by Hardiman and published as *A Chorographical Description of West or h-Iar Connaught* by the Dublin Archæological Society in 1846.) Margaret, who plays an important part in the romantic story of the origin of the Claddagh ring, was the daughter of John Joyce – O'Flaherty refers to her as Margaret Joyce Fitz-John – and so a member of the 'tribe' that is most closely connected with the elusive ring.

In July 1601, Sir Oliver Lambart, the newly-appointed governor of Connacht, improved the fortifications of the city of Galway, a significant move in the year of Kinsale. By the time Charles I was being challenged by the forces of Parliament the city ranked as one of Ireland's most important and wealthiest towns. The Tribes were by attitude Royalist and as Catholics were natural candidates for membership of the Catholic Confederacy, which they joined in 1642. Ten years later their city fell to Cromwell's soldiers under the younger Coote after a nine-month land-and-sea blockade, and in 1655 the inhabitants were ordered to leave the town as a prelude to a plantation which never in fact took place. With the Restoration of

Charles II in 1660 and the later appointment of Richard Talbot, Earl of Tyrconnell, as Viceroy by Charles's brother James II in 1687, the city regained some of its old prosperity but its instinctive support for the Jacobite forces meant that it was on the losing side again during the Williamite wars. On 21 July 1691 it surrendered to Ginkel and its years of glory were over. The town was left bereft of its leaders and reverted to a low-level life that characterised most centres of Catholic population during the eighteenth century. Yet in 1762 of a total population of 14,000 only 350 were Protestant and the old mercantile spirit of the town had begun to surface again. The Galway merchants had agents in Dublin, London, Nantes and Bordeaux, and links with Spain and Mediterranean countries stayed strong.

The final blow to the town's spirit and one which seemed to mark the end of its career as the mercantile jewel of the West was the great Famine of 1846-7. As the only sizeable town between Derry and Limerick it bore the burden of the care of refugees and its urban population was decimated by the typhus and other pestilences associated with the catastrophe. Captain Hellard, the Poor Law inspector for the city, reported in 1847 that 'no less than eleven boats loaded with destitute persons' had come into Galway Harbour from Connemara, 'most from the estate of Christian St George, our county member, who I am told is ejecting them without a rag to cover them.' In spite of deaths from starvation and disease the population by 1851 had doubled to 23,695. The 1901 figure of 16,257 is an index of the slow decline in the town in the post-Famine years, just as its present population of in excess of

40,000 clearly indicates it cultural and economic buoyancy.

With the coming of the railways and better roads the city became again the significant distribution centre of its large hinterland. It was the port of departure for the Aran Islands and played its part in the emigration that was responsible to a greater degree than Famine deaths for halving the country's population. It was significant in the Gaelic League's recovery of the Irish language, supplying one of its best-loved writers in Padraic Ó Conaire (1882–1928), and it is fitting that it should be the home of *Taibhdhearc na Gaillimhe*, the theatre where all the plays produced are in Irish. Many of the great names of the Irish Literary Renaissance, Edward Martyn, George Moore, Lady Gregory, came from the region that has the city as its capital, and even before their work began, the city's two theatres and temperance hall made its citizens 'familiar with the works of Shakespeare, Sheridan and Goldsmith' as Pádraig Ó Laoi records in his *Nora Barnacle Joyce* (1982).

In fact the later history of Galway is a kind of reversal of its traditions. From being a non-Gaelic town in a solid Gaeltacht it became the most Irish of the larger towns of Ireland. It was the place where in Eyre Square on a Saturday night you were as likely to hear Irish as English. Robert Lynd (1879–1949), the essayist, visited it in 1912 during Race Week (the Tuesday, Wednesday and Thursday preceding the first Monday of August) and found it the most Irish of cities:

> Historians of the old-fashioned sort tell you that Galway is not an Irish city. It is true enough that it

first appears on the records after the Normans had come to it with their energetic genius for towns and systems. But nothing remains of the Normans now save dust and stones. It was in vain that they wrote up on the western gate of this medieval fortress the fantastic prayer: 'From the fury of the O'Flaherties, good Lord, deliver us.' The O'Flaherties, or what the O'Flaherties stand for, are its supreme distinction now. (*Rambles in Ireland*)

Lynd was famous for being an Ulster Presbyterian Nationalist and with his dry sense of humour he would have been very pleased to learn that unferocious O'Flahertys became mayors in 1951 and 1964.

The chapter from which this excerpt was taken was entitled 'Galway of the Races' a neat pun on the city's usual historical blazon. The races kept and keep Galway's name in the public eye, as this anonymous early nineteenth-century broadsheet rhyme 'Galway Races' celebrates:

It's there you'll see confectioners with sugar sticks
and dainties,
The lozenges and oranges, lemonade and raisins;
The gingerbread and spices to accommodate the
ladies,
And a big crubeen for threepence to be picking
while you're able.

It's there you'll see the gamblers, the thimbles and
the garters,

And the sporting Wheel of Fortune with the four
and twenty quarters,
There was others without scruple pelting wattles at
poor Maggy,
And her father well contented and he looking at his
daughter.

It's there you'll see the pipers and fiddlers com-
peting,
And the nimble-footed dancers and they tripping
on the daisies.
There was others crying segars and lights, and the
bill of all the races,
With the colour of the jockeys, the prize and
horses' ages.

It's there you'll see the jockeys and they mounted
on most stately,
The pink and blue, the red and green, the Emblem
of our nation.
When the bell was rung for starting, the horses
seemed impatient,
Though they never stood on ground, their speed
was so amazing.

There was half a million people there of all denomi-
nations,
The Catholic, the Protestant, the Jew and Presbyterian.
There was yet no animosity, no matter what persua-
sion,

But *fáilte* and hospitality, inducing fresh acquaint-
ance.

The modern city (incorporated as a county borough in
1986, the first Irish city to receive this status this century)
can justly claim to be as distinctive and as colourful a
small city as any in Europe. The old attitudes which made
it as soundly commercial as Birmingham and as exotic as
Samarkand in the past have been shown not to have died
out in its twilight centuries but to have awakened from a
long sleep. The Queen's College that was the first sign of
hope when it opened in 1848 is now a large university
college, and town and gown combine to make it the most
fascinating place in Ireland, after Dublin, and a necessary
resort for the ever-growing numbers of tourists. It is no
longer true, as in Mary Devenport O'Neill's poem quoted
earlier that 'there time goes slow' nor do 'their tall houses
crumble away', but there is no doubt that

> This town is eaten through with memory
> Of pride and thick red Spanish wine and gold
> And a great come and go.

It is search of that gold that we must now go.

2

WHERE THE 'CLADDAGH' ROLLS DOWN TO THE SEA

Long before the city was built the fishing village of the 'shore' was already in existence. (The song by P. B. Kelly which places the site as where 'the Claddagh rolls down to the sea' uses a little bit of forgivable balladeer's licence. The river that joins the bay there is the source of both city and village, the Galway river, whatever the origin of its name may be.) The inhabitants were Irish-speaking and the village, though for many centuries part of the town if actually outside the barbican wall, enjoyed an even greater autonomy than did the tribal families. The *cladach* would have made a suitable landing place for the earliest keel-less craft. (At the beginning of this century the place was famous for the number of open and half-decked sailing smacks called *púcáin* and *gleoiteoga* that vanished with the Claddagh in the mid-1930s.) As far as fishing grounds were concerned the men of the Claddagh claimed exclusive rights over the whole of the bay. In the heyday there were about 150 sailboats and 100 rowing boats, used mainly for netting herring. The sturdily independent denizens were also noted for their conservatism. Hardiman in his history of Galway notes that

> ... though they sometimes exhibit a great shew of industry, they are still so wedded to old customs, that they invariably eject, with the most inveterate prejudice, any new improvement in their fishing apparatus, which is consequently now very little superior to that used centuries ago by their ancestors. The consequence is, that the great mass of wealth which here lies engulfed in the bosom of the deep has been hitherto but partially explored; and the riches which yearly flow into this extensive inlet are suffered again to depart, through the indolence, and sometimes superstitious prejudices, of this otherwise useful and meritorious body of men. When they do not themselves think proper to fish, they invariably prevent any other from attempting it, viewing, with all the monopolizing spirit of any corporation, the bay as their exclusive domain, on which to use their own words, they never admit any trespasser; and, therefore, should a single boat from any other district venture out to fish, without the concurrence of the Claddagh body, it does so at the risk of being destroyed.

Another commentator, Samuel Lewis, who published *A Topographical Dictionary of Ireland* in 1837, comments:

> For the protection of those who attempted to fish against the regulations of the Claddagh fishermen,

a gun-ship was stationed in the bay some few years since, during which time the object was attained; but on its removal the fishermen again enforced their authority, and now exercise an uncontrolled power of preventing others from fishing in the bay in opposition to their peculiar regulation.

These peculiar regulations were maintained even during the Famine: the fishermen maintained their right to off-days and would, as always, permit no one else to fish in their waters, whatever the occasion.

All visitors who made the journey to Galway found it necessary to comment upon the oddity of the Claddagh. Henry D. Inglis in his *Ireland in 1834* is anxious to record his impressions:

> The people of the Claddagh are perfect exclusives. They live intensely among themselves – seldom leave the Claddagh, unless merely to take their fish to market; hold no intercourse with townspeople; and marry entirely among each other. The *tocher* [dowry] brought by a girl on her marriage is generally the share of a boat.

Eighty years later Stephen Gwynn (1864-1950) found surprisingly little changed but could not help notice that even there the modern age was beginning to have an effect. In his book *The Famous Cities of Ireland* (1915) he wrote:

> The Claddagh is to-day what it has always been –

an Irish-speaking village, lying outside the limits of the city proper, and living its life apart. Outside every Anglo-Norman town there grew up an 'Irish town' beyond the walls, beyond the city pale; and at Galway its people were fishers, who have probably, since the beginning of time, complained that 'the fish are not in it as they used to be'. At all events, a bye-law of 1585 enacted that no fisherman 'do take in hand the ploughe or spade that would barr them from fishing.' But if the harvester of the sea was forbidden to seek labour on the land or in the town, the community recognised that the fisher needed help in his precarious job; and they enacted that fishers or their wives 'be reasonably served before others with all necessary sustenance and food, whereby they might have the better hope.' Today in Galway, as anywhere else, there is complaint of the trawlers; and now the local sailing trawlers, of which the Claddagh complains, are, in their turn, complaining of the steam trawlers which sweep their grounds mercilessly. The Claddagh men, or the older of them, cling to their old, high-sided boats, beautiful sea-craft; yet side by side with these you will find the larger flush-decked 'nobbies' [called this from their shape] and 'Zulus' [two-masted vessels originally from northeast Scotland, established there at the time of the Zulu war (1878–9)] which the Congested Districts Board have introduced on the Connemara shore and in Aran. Claddagh has never taken kindly to these; but it has gone a step beyond them, and a motor boat,

the *Claddagh King*, now follows the sign of the herring all round the Irish coast.

As with many another antique curiosity, interest in preservation came too late. The charming oddity of the place and the notion of its uniqueness, which fascinated visitors in the past and to which tribute was regularly paid by the travel writers of the time, had disappeared by 1934. With the coming of the new state the city's recovery was accelerated and considerations other than the picturesque had priority with the city fathers. The higgledy-piggledy network of streets and lanes that formed the Claddagh – Hardiman describes it as 'irregularly built but very extensive, and intersected into several streets' – and the primitive hygienic arrangements were deemed 'unhealthy' in 1927, and by 1934 brick and cement had replaced the older building materials. Gone were the mud-walled huts with thatched roofs and in their place 'arrays of unsightly concrete houses' (as the *Shell Guide* (1989) rather acidly puts it) were built. Lost too was the intricate structure of self-government that made the village from time immemorial a kind of independent entity, which had an uneasy relationship with the most independent of Irish towns.

Even in this century St John's Day (24 June) was a significant date, when the Claddagh folk elected mayor, sheriff and other civic officers, and the election was followed by a ceremonial procession through the town. The whole village turned out dressed in their finery, the women in blue and red with cotton headscarves, the men in blue unbuttoned knee-breeches, white flannel vests, blue jackets and broad-brimmed hats, with red silk scarves round their necks. Precedence was important, the order of the procession being determined by the mayor. A special feature were the poles surmounted by local emblems which were carried by young men in short white jackets with silk sashes and wearing hats ornamented with ribbons and flowers. The parade was led by a band and became an important part of the Galway summer. Interestingly the same kind of rout is held yearly on 8 May in the west Cornish town of Helston. The Helston Furry is pre-Christian in origin and is traditionally a dancing celebration of the town's survival of an attack by a dragon. It is likely that the Claddagh merrymaking was a form of thanksgiving for safety during the last fishing season and propitiation for the one to come.

The mayor's boat was distinguishable by a white flag and sails instead of the usual brown or black, and the start of the fishing season was marked by a formal ceremony which consisted of a simultaneous casting and drawing of nets from the assembled fleet. Later, as in Tory Island, another quasi-independent republic, the head of government was vested in a king who was granted the same visible privileges including the arrogated title of admiral of the bay. The last King of the Claddagh, Eoin Concannon, died aged ninety in 1954. Because of the autonomous nature of the settlement, with intermarriage the norm, and its innate conservatism, the characteristic folkways remained unchanged for centuries. It is not known when the people of the Claddagh adopted the ring that bears its name but the persistence of its usage throughout some terrible times is entirely appropriate.

It was a place devoted to fish and fishing, the men the finders and the women the disposers of the catch. Often they carried their wares on wide flat baskets balanced on folds of shawls on their heads so that their hands might be free. Even knitting was possible, so steady were the 'skibs' and so erect the carriers. By the end of the eighteenth century the Claddagh men supplied the city and the districts around with their main source of food. From 1750 until at least 1840 the number of local boats fishing the bay never dropped below 200. Arthur Young in his *A Tour in Ireland* (1780) noted that demand was always greater than supply, and fish from other ports had to be brought in. He put this down to the eccentric work-schedule of the Claddagh men who 'far from being industrious, some weeks ... do not go out twice'. Hely Dutton in his *Survey* (1824) is a bit scathing about the arbitrariness of the mayor's power. He is irritated by his seeming delay in allowing herring catches to begin, especially since every gull from Clare to Mayo knew they had arrived:

When it is his [the admiral's] pleasure, an evening is appointed, and all the boats assemble at the Cloddagh [sic], near Galway, or meet them on the way to the amount of 500 or upwards, and all sail out together, and preserve a profound silence until they arrive at the fishing ground; and a charming sight it is. Upon a signal given by the admiral's boat, they all drop their nets. As the great scull of herrings divide shortly after they enter the bay, and fill every creek and inlet of it, much time is lost by this nonsensical and tyrannical parade, for it is well known by the owners of small boats in those creeks many days before the admiral signifies his great and mighty pleasure, but they dare not fish.

In their *Hand-books for Ireland: The West and Connamara* (1853) Anna Hall (1800-81) and her husband Samuel (1800-89), those indefatigable travellers and sketch-writers, recorded their fascination with the 'colony of fishermen' who numbered 'with their families, between four and five thousand.' (This was an updated offprint from their magisterial three-volume *Ireland, Its Scenery, Character, &c* which was published in 1842.) Their illustration of the marketplace shows it as close to the Spanish Arch and outside their own 'dominion'.

'Their own dominion' it may be called literally, for they are governed by their own king and their own laws; and it is difficult, if not impossible, to make them obedient to any other.

The Claddagh is a populous district lying to the right of the harbour, consisting of streets, squares, and lanes; all inhabited by fishermen. They claim the right to exercise complete and exclusive control over the bay, and, indeed, over all the bays of the county. They are peaceable and industrious, and their cottages are cleaner and better furnished than most of the Galway dwellings; but if any of the 'rights' they have enjoyed for centuries are infringed, they become so violent that nothing can withstand them.

They go on to describe an event which occurred during their visit in 1845 and illustrated not only the persistence of the superstitions but the violent sanctions that the Claddagh people could impose if these beliefs were ignored or their authority questioned. A gentleman 'determining to break through this absurd custom, which left the town without fish for days together, ventured to man his own boat; and well manned and well armed he set forth on his voyage.' Reaction was instant; the men of the Claddagh who had been quietly engaged on net-mending and keel-scraping, as they did on these 'unlucky' days, put to sea, also 'well armed', and 'a chase commenced likely to terminate in the destruction of the enterprising man who dared to dispute the 'ould ancient laws of the Claddagh'.' He was lucky to escape with his life, 'his cool bravery' saving him 'during a precipitate retreat.'

They were full of praise for the 'king', who once a 'veritable despot' was 'now nothing more than the Lord Mayor of Dublin, or any other city'.

> He has still, however, much influence, and sacrifices himself, literally without fee or reward, for 'the good of the people': he is constantly occupied hearing and deciding causes and quarrels, for his people never, by any chance, appeal to a higher tribunal.

They finish their account with the regret that on their latest visit they found 'the interesting suburb much deteriorated'. The Famine had had a severe effect: 'many of the cabins, neat and orderly a few years before, had become dilapidated' and the placed swarmed with beggars. With their unerring eye for the picturesque in the places they visited it was natural that they should mention the 'wedding-ring' of the 'quarter' and provide an illustration of the characteristic hand-clasped crowned heart. What they couldn't know was that many of these precious heirlooms had been pawned in Galway to help pay for passages to America, without any real hope of redemption.

The religious needs of the people of the Claddagh were met by Dominicans rather than by secular clergy. They first arrived in 1488 and continued to minister until Cromwellian times, when their foundation suffered severe damage. This was due partly to bombardment by Parliamentary forces and partly to a kind of scorched earth policy recommended by the city's Royalist commanders in 1652, by which the monks agreed to the demolition of their church in case its sturdy structure should provide a stronghold for the assailants. The site of the new church built after the Restoration, also called St Mary's, has survived to the present day. The Dominicans and their flock weathered the Williamite war and the Penal century, and the monks were at the forefront in the nineteenth-century agitation for a school for the people of the Claddagh.

The story is told in detail in an excellent monograph by Alf MacLochlainn, who many years later filled the same post as the city's great historian, James Hardiman. He was the first librarian of the Queen's College, Galway, having refused the chair of Irish. In 'The origins and early history of the Claddagh Piscatory School' in *Two Galway Schools* (1993) MacLochlainn makes it clear that it was due to the efforts of a number of Dominican fathers, especially T. R. Rushe, that government recommendations made in 1837 were put into practice. A prior report by a Galway fishing committee deprecated 'the absence for many years of education in this populous colony' which had led 'to early and improvident marriages whereby a population has grown ignorant of the English language and such training as might enable its numerous children to inter-marry with the surrounding people or fit them for situations in the Navy or merchant vessels'. This down-grading of Irish by education was common countrywide and increased greatly in the years immediately after the Famine. Poor and not so poor Irish-speaking parents acquiesced in this rooting out of Irish in their children, for the best, as they saw it, of economic reasons.

It was in 1846 that Fr Rush made his appeal and his letter proposed that the Piscatory School should encour-age the introduction of new fishing techniques and impart 'to many of the youth of the Claddagh . . . a good Nautical Education.' By 1848 he was able to report that 'although they are not in operation for more than twelve months [the schools] have a daily attendance of more than 400 boys and girls.' Though in the first decade of its existence the girls made sails, ropes and nets, the nautical, indeed, the piscatorial, ambitions of the founders were never fully realised and by 1887 it was functioning as an ordinary national school. The memory of its marine associations was enshrined in the statue of a mariner on the cornice above the main door.

Fish and fishing remained the business and the rationale of the village and it became an annual custom for the fleet to be blessed by the priests of St Mary's. (Up till the 1830s an older *piseóg* required the burial of a cat in the strand as a means of obtaining fair winds.) The Blessing of the Bay, inaugurated around 1835, meant that the power of the Christian religion was added to the older beliefs. On a chosen Sunday in mid-August the smacks were guided into position round a craft holding the priest and his acolytes. The place chosen was to the west of the little Mutton Island about two miles south of the city. There a blessing was asked on all the fleet that good catches, especially of herring, would characterise the season. At the time of the inauguration of the blessing there would have been hundreds of boats; in 1941 the number was eighteen. The blessing is still carried out, a worthy if symbolic survival of past glory, but when the fleet assembled on 15 August 1993, of the ten boats present only two were survivors of the old fleet of sailboats. (For this as for many other details of Claddagh lore I am deeply indebted to what must be the standard and indispensable work for many years to come, *Down by the Claddagh* (1993) by Peadar O'Dowd.)

The Claddagh is now a dream, a remarkable community that could not survive the uniformity of the twentieth century. There is a Latin tag which states: *Corpora lente augescunt; cito extinguuntur* – 'Bodies are slow to grow but quick to decay.' In its golden age in the years before the Famine of the 1840s and again before the intrusion of the state, the Claddagh had an envied and jealously preserved autonomy. The most extensive account of the way of life of its people which could be taken as true in its essentials for most of the village's existence, is that of Hardiman, even though most of it is given in a footnote as long as a chapter. It is worth quoting at length because of its excellent style and its carefully researched history. The book was published in 1820 and some of the information contained is fascinating. The returns of the most recent census, that of 1812, showed that there were 468 houses, all thatched, 'inhabited by 500 families, consisting of 1050 males and 1286 females', (life expectancy in the male being less even in those conditions). He believes that the population at the time of writing is 'considerably greater, being supposed to exceed 3000 souls'.

He praises the people's capacity to read the bay and know when to put to sea, and is impressed by their industry at home:

When on shore they are principally employed in attending to, and repairing their boats, sails, rigging, cordage, &c, and in making, drying or repairing their nets and spillets [lines], in which latter employment they are generally assisted by the women, who spin the hemp and yarn for the nets. In consequence of their strict attention to these particulars very few accidents happen at sea, and lives are seldom lost among them.

He is properly impressed by what he calls their 'internal regulations' and has the same praise for the mayor as had the Halls. When he speaks about the people's lack of politics you can sense his own envy of their happy lot:

> [The mayor] regulates the community according to
> their own peculiar laws and customs, and settles
> all their fishery disputes. His decisions are so
> decisive, and so much respected, that the parties
> are seldom known to carry their differences before
> a legal tribunal, or to trouble the civil magistrates.
> They neither understand nor trouble themselves
> about politics, consequently in the most turbulent
> times their loyalty has never been questioned, and
> they are exempt from all government taxes.

The essence of the Claddagh is to be found here in
Hardiman's summary. The life described had altered little
from what it was in the past and it continued without
significant change. A palpable sense of centuries of
tradition and an idiosyncratic way of life seems to have
affected many modern visitors. They claimed to experi-
ence it even in the much reduced village that was finally
incorporated in the city from which it had stood so calmly
aloof. Most visitors to Galway at any time up to the mid-
1930s made a visit as a matter of course, and no professional traveller could afford to miss it. Stephen Gwynn
was a regular pilgrim and in his book *A Holiday in
Connemara* (1909) he argues that the inhabitants of the
Claddagh are direct descendants of the pre-Celtic Firbolgs,
'that older race who built the great dun of Aran'. Their
lack of interest in politics which so struck Hardiman was
still a characteristic:

... to the Claddagh man you can only talk about the Claddagh; Ireland has no appeal to him. The land question does not touch him for he has no land; the revival of fisheries along the coast has done him no good, for he was catching fish before, and he has his own sufficient market ...

Henry Vollam Morton (1892–1979), another traveller, who wrote *In Search of Ireland* (1930), the most famous of all pre-war accounts of what was still called the Emerald Isle, saw it in its long twilight and found it as fascinating as did any of his predecessors:

Nothing is more picturesque ... than this astonishing fishing village of neat whitewashed, thatched cottages planted at haphazard angles with no regular roads running to them. If you took three hundred little toy cottages and jumbled them on a nursery floor you would have something like the Claddagh. It is a triumph of unconscious beauty.

At night the Claddagh is most beautiful. There are no street lamps. You find your way through the maze of houses by the light that falls through windows and open doors. The path of earth has been beaten hard by the feet of generations going back to the Norman conquest of Ireland. The lime-washed houses with the peat reek coming from their chimneys shine in the half light. The children who in daylight play on the squares of beaten earth and before the cabin doors have been put to bed. It is quiet and watchful and full of the chirping of crickets.

The sense of loss, of a glory departed, is strong. The Claddagh exists now only in books, pictures, song and the memory of the people. A lot is known about its history and more will be garnered. Yet no matter how much becomes established about the people and their unique way of life they hold their secrets still. No one has penetrated the heart of their mystery. It is ironic that their likely memorial will be the ring that they, or somebody else, named after their remarkable village.

3

'What Shall We Do for a Ring?'

The circle as a symbol has always had great power. In magic it is a figure of great strength, having no corners where weakness could show or contrary spirits lurk. As a wheel it shares only one point with the ground and so is usefully unstable. The circle is a clear sign of eternity since it is endless, and therefore when it takes the form of a ring it is a suitable symbol of constancy. The ring's sexual symbolism, too, is clear enough not to require further comment and its convenience for wearing made it a popular form of personal decoration, for both men and women, since at least the fourth millennium BC.

The first rings were simple circlets of gold or silver. (The use of baser metals was not common until the coming of the Industrial Revolution in the eighteenth century and the invention of such alloys as pinchbeck (83 per cent copper to 17 per cent zinc) which gave a passable simulation of gold. Its name came from its inventor Christopher Pinchbeck (1670–1732), a Fleet Street jeweller who used it to cover the cases of pocket watches.) The earliest rings of the Celts were of this kind with decorations made repoussé-style by hammering relief designs from the back. Chasing, the pushing aside of metal to make a mark without loss of the precious material, such as happens with engraving, was also common with the early artificers. Much earlier in time women are known to have worn finger-rings of silver, as archæological discoveries in Mesopotamia have proved. During the Sumerian civilisation (c. 3500–350bc) rings were a normal part of ceremonial ornamentation. Grave remains suggest that it was only royalty, kings, queens and their families, and the highest members of the priestly castes, who could afford to own them. They were not heirlooms, in the sense that ownership belonged to the family and was the possession of the heir only during his or her lifetime; these were personal possessions of the dead person and, like their unfortunate body-servants, were buried with them.

The civilisation of Ancient Egypt, contemporary with that of Sumeria but lasting till about AD300, had similar ornamentation and the same practice of burying personal possessions with the mummified bodies of their aristocratic owners. Rings were regularly used in the kingdom instead of coins. The Greeks of classical antiquity tended not to wear rings as decorations (similar gaps in their use occurred around 2500bc) and it wasn't until the time of the Romans that the ring became more than just a decoration or sign of position or authority. In the days of the Republic (c. 500–27bc) and more widely in the Western Empire (until c. AD500) rings had an important social significance. Freeborn citizens were permitted to wear an iron ring but only senators and chief magistrates, and in the later empire the *equites* (the members of the

Equestrian Order who took power from the Senate) enjoyed the *ius annuli aurei*, the right to wear a ring of gold. The emperors reserved the right to grant the privilege to whom they pleased and the long-lived Byzantine emperor Justinian (*c.* 482–565) conferred the title on all Roman citizens. Though they still served as badges of office, their use as talismans or lucky charms increased. Roman rings usually had bezels, strips of metal to hold a projecting decoration or gemstone. Sometimes the bezel had the owner's mark or signet done in intaglio (engraved) so that the impression on the wax would stand in relief. In the later empire common bezel decorations were gold-knots or coins. One such survival is a strong torus band holding a coin which shows the head of Faustina, the wife of the Emperor Antoninus Pius (AD86–161). As the empire grew richer and, its critics said, more decadent, rings became very popular with many of the middle class Romans who served the *imperium Romanum* from Scotland to the Nile. One man is reported to have worn six rings on each finger!

Solitaire rings were popular, usually with cabochon (polished but uncut) stones or with engraved bezels, sometimes heart-shaped or showing intricate knots. With the increase of their use as a normal part of the formal dress of the comfortably-off a kind of mute language of significance grew up around them. Worn on the forefinger the ring signified power, whereas wearing rings on the little finger was a sign of affection. In the lore of our Claddagh ring the significance of the way it was worn is crucial to the story.

What modern brides and grooms owe to the Romans

of the later empire, however, is the engagement and the wedding ring. Rings were first exchanged as marks of betrothal, usual both as decorations and as a sign of unavailablity. Their bestowal had no especial religious significance, being merely a secular gesture. Their use as wedding bands came later. From this period, too, is dated the posy ring, one with a sentimental inscription on the inside, so that the message would be hidden from the curious eye and be known only to the giver, the recipient and their intimates. The word is a shortened form of 'poesy' or 'poetry' and refers to the verse or motto inscribed. Common mottos were *Semper Amemus* ('Let us love forever,' or less sanguinely, 'May we love forever') and *αει* the Greek word for 'always'. The idea of the internal inscription has continued to the present day in wedding rings or eternity rings, usually consisting of the names of the loving parties and the date of their wedding. Posies were most popular from the sixteenth century to the end of the eighteenth. They usually expressed undying love and had such inscriptions as 'For ever and for aye'; 'In thee my choice, I do rejoice'; 'When this you see, Then think of me'; 'Love is heaven, and heaven is love'; 'Not two but one Till life is gone'. The banality of the sentiment expressed and the poor quality of the verse caused the posies to be mocked by the more intellectual members of society. When Hamlet hears the rhyming prologue to the travelling players' production of *The Mousetrap*:

For us and for our tragedy
Here stooping to your clemency
We beg your hearing patiently

he jibes, 'Is this a prologue, or the posy of a ring?'

One common posy, 'My heart and I, Until I die' marks the ring as a special kind, also dating from Roman times. This motto was used for a special design of ring called a *fede* (Italian from the Roman word *fides* meaning 'faith'). Plain rings without bezels were usually decorated round the outside with palmette leaves which were shaped like hearts. The bezelled ring had two hands clasped to represent *mani in fede*, 'hands in faith'. These two elements of design come nicely together in the ring which is the object of our search.

The ring continued to play its part in people's lives, even in what used incorrectly to be called the 'dark ages', the period between the fall of the Roman Empire and the coming of the New Learning at the Renaissance. At a time when literacy was despised by the European chieftains and rulers who gained power after the end of *pax Romana* the intaglio ring was the usual means of signature. The Vikings who were the scourge of northern Europe between the eighth and eleventh centuries used gold rings as easily carried, realisable capital when they combined piracy with aggressive merchandising in their rather vigorous immigrant policy. In more settled times rings were used as tokens of membership of the various medieval craft guilds.

When England settled to a comparative peace under the Tudors early in the sixteenth century there was a great demand for gorgeous decoration, and jewellery-making enjoyed a boom. Henry VIII had no fewer than thirty-nine heart-shaped brooches. One heart-shaped pendant dating from the period is now part of the collection of Elizabeth

II. A central sapphire is hinged at the side and may be opened to reveal a pair of clasped hands, in *fede* style. The heart is surmounted by a crown which also opens to reveal two hearts joined in a knot. It is interesting that the constituent elements of the Claddagh ring should be present together in a much older piece. The heart was becoming a common bezel-decoration and it often concealed a secret compartment as in a neck locket. This might contain favours like locks of hair, cameo miniatures of lovers and, for the purposes of melodrama, poison in powder form.

The plain gold ring continued to be the mark of the married woman, although its modern position on the third finger of the left hand dates only from the end of the sixteenth century. Until that date the wedding band was worn on the third finger of the right hand, the usual position for ceremonial rings or symbols of authority. Cardinals, bishops and abbots wore gold rings there, with sapphires for their eminences and amethysts for the others. The pope wears his several rings on the same finger, the most famous being the Ring of the Fisherman with which he is invested at his election and which is broken up at his death. Nuns at final profession wear the plain gold band of the spouse, and the Doge of Venice used to throw a gold ring into the Adriatic on Ascension Thursday to assert that the city is the Bride of the Sea.

It is in fable and legend that the ring of all other pieces of decoration comes into its own. In the Arabian Nights story of Aladdin, the Genie of the Ring is only slightly less powerful than that of the more famous Lamp. Gyges, the remote and certainly entirely mythical ancestor of the Lydian kings who is said to have reigned in the seventh century BC, found a ring on a giant's corpse which could make him invisible if he turned the bezel inwards, a trick which helped him greatly in his career. Solomon's ring enabled him to overcome all opponents, to transport himself to the celestial spheres where he learned the secrets of the universe and it also enabled him to talk to and understand the members of the animal kingdom. Polycrates, the tyrant of Samos, a man of famous good fortune, was advised to throw a precious ring into the sea so as not to incur the wrath of the gods, but found it in a fish which was served to him a few days later. King Edward the Confessor once gave a ring as alms to an old beggar. Some English pilgrims to the Holy Land met the same old man who said he was St John the Evangelist and asked them to take the ring back to 'Saint' Edward. Sir Owain, one of the Knights of the Round Table, was given a ring which had the same effect as Gyges's ring. So long as the bezel-stone was concealed, so was its wearer. In Irish folklore rings were often used as means of identification and sometimes they had the magical property of providing the wearer with food and drink, as a protection against accepting hospitality from strangers and thereby coming into their power.

One of the most significant examples of the symbolic power of rings is given in the story of the Ring of Innocent. On 29 May 1205 Pope Innocent III (1160-1216) sent King John of England, a man he was soon to excommunicate, four gold rings set with precious stones. Their circular shape signified eternity ('Remember we are all passing through time into eternity'); their number signified the four cardinal virtues: prudence, justice, temperance and fortitude; the material stood for 'wisdom from on high, which is as gold purified in the fire'; the emerald was the emblem of faith, the sapphire of hope, the garnet of charity and the topaz of good works.

In Elizabethan times the wearing of *memento mori* rings with a skull and crossbones was common, as were memorial rings. Shakespeare when he died as a rich burgher of Stratford left 26s 8d (a considerable sum of money) apiece to buy memorial rings for three actor friends, Richard Burbage, John Heminges and Henry Condell, and for four Stratford pals, Hamnet Sadler, William Reynolds and the brothers Anthony and John Nash. The practice of wearing memorial rings, often with hairs of the dead person woven into the gold of the bezel, was common in Wales until the early twentieth century. Another ring design which dates from the late sixteenth century was the gemmel or gimmel ring (from *gemellus,* a Latin word meaning 'little twin'). As the name implies it had two parts which could be worn separately, each with a hand on the bezel. But when the two pieces were worn together the hands were seen to clasp.

The history of rings then is very ancient and few new ideas about structure have been contrived in recent times. Even the knuckleduster, that modern item of attack and defence that covers the fingers and welds together four rings with a single long bezel, was anticipated by the Elizabethan dandies who wore double rings that held the middle and ring fingers together. The elements of the Claddagh ring clearly existed before they came to be assembled so strikingly in eighteenth-century Galway.

4

—

THE CLADDAGH RING

As with many other things Irish, in trying to discover the true origins of the Claddagh ring the difficulty lies in separating marvellous myths from fairly dull reality. The best technical account of its origins is that given by Ida Delamer in an article published in the *Irish Arts Review Yearbook* (Vol 12, 1996). She identifies it as a *fede* ring, the clasped hand motif having been 'in use on bezels of love rings since Roman times'. Her description, 'a plain hoop attached to a hammered or cast bezel designed as two hands clasping a crowned heart', shows the ring to have affinities with one dated 1706, which is part of the collection of the Victoria and Albert Museum in London. This is in essence a more elaborate, gaudier version of the standard design, with the heart a diamond stone and the clasping hands done in enamel. It has an inner inscription: 'Dudley and Katherine united 26 Mar 1706' and it is in Ms Delamer's opinion a wedding ring.

The earliest of the Irish rings of the Claddagh type are of the same date (*c.* 1700) and of the four that exist only one can be attributed to the man generally credited with its devising, Richard Joyce (*fl.* 1690–1737) of Galway; the others are reliably assigned to a goldsmith named Thomas Meade who lived in Kinsale from 1689 until 1730. The Joyce ring has the initials NCM and MRC inscribed on the inside as well as RI, the mark of the maker. As Ms Delamer's article makes clear, the motif of two hands clasping a crowned heart was also incorporated into the presidential chair of the Kinsale Knot of the Society of Friendly Brothers. The chair was made about 1760 and had beneath the 'Claddagh' motif the motto *Quis Separbit* (correctly *separabit*), the whole meaning 'Who will separate (us)'.

It is not clear whether Meade's successors in Kinsale continued to make rings with the 'Claddagh' insignia but judging by jewellers' marks, most of the extant rings were made in Galway. The punches of the goldsmiths George Robinson and Austin French are to be found on many rings that belong to the years 1770-1800. (The latter may very well have had a family connection with Richard Joyce, since one of Joyce's daughters married Andrew Roe French.) Other Galway jewellers who contributed to the gradual extension of what we may call the Claddagh ring industry were Andrew Robinson, Nicholas Burgh, James Clinch and James Sealy, though the rings did not become associated with the Claddagh village until well into the nineteenth century.

One of the reasons for the assigning of the Galway ring to the Claddagh was the enthusiasm of the Halls in their travel book mentioned earlier. They illustrated their account with an engraving of the ring and gave this description of Claddagh marriage customs:

The wedding ring is an heir-loom in a family. It is regularly transferred by the mother to her daughter first married; and so on to their descendants. The rings are large, of solid gold, and not unfrequently cost from two to three pounds each.

In a footnote they state:

They are very similar in character to the 'Gimmal Ring' with which our ancestors of the reign of Elizabeth and earlier 'made an end of wooing.' These ancient rings (like the Galway ones) were formed into the shape of two hands, a heart being placed in each palm. It was, however, constructed of twin or double hoops, as its name imports, which was derived from the Latin *gemellus,* or French *jumeau;* the course of the twist in each hoop being made to correspond with that of its counterpart, so that on bringing them together, they united in one ring, forming an emblem of married life, and the hands conjoined in the centre. The Galway rings are single throughout, but a strong analogy is perceptible, the rudeness of their construction precluding the neatness and ingenuity displayed in the elder – if it be the elder – prototype.

The Halls' industry – Anna is credited with 500 books – and their popularity with their English readers can hardly be overestimated. The Ireland they presented was the one that was acceptable, and to be fair they gave a reasonably truthful if selective picture. Naturally the folksy, even cosy elements were the popular ones, and British armchair tourists seized on the pleasant eccentricity of the existence of such a place as the Claddagh. When so recognisable and romantic an artefact as the ring could be associated with an idiosyncratic and independent fishing community it was bound to become a talking point. The ghost of Sir Walter Scott and the predilection of Queen Victoria for tartans and highland bonnets worn in Balmoral Castle, had made plaid kilts and kirtles very much the mode in contemporary London. Earlier Tom Moore had sung of minstrel boys and harps and presented a romantic Ireland that eased the English liberal conscience. (It is no coincidence that the Halls were later responsible for setting up a memorial to Moore in the village of Bromham in Wiltshire where he was buried in 1852.) Romantic Ireland, a kind of *doppelganger* of the distressful, unsettled country, was born, and it survived to provide Dion Boucicault with audiences for the melodramas which made great use of ruined castles, shamrocks and beautiful Irish colleens. This elaborately designed ring was just the sort of thing to catch the fashionable imagination.

The Halls are not to blame, however, for calling it the Claddagh ring; they referred to it simply as the *Galway* ring, but the placing of the engraving on the same page as their description of 'this primitive suburb' in a book with a wide circulation had the inevitable and commercially useful effect of naming it forever. The name of Thomas Crofton Croker (1798–1854) is also associated with the surge in its popularity. Croker was born in Cork and worked as a clerk with the Admiralty from the age of twenty until his retirement in 1850. He did for Munster what Scott did for the Borders, collecting and publishing much folklore in ballads and traditional stories. His tendency to 'improve' the stories and make them more like 'literature', and his generally unscholarly approach, have left him open to criticism, but his contribution to *béaloideas* at a time of linguistic and social change was invaluable. Mutual friends of Moore, the Halls used Croker as one of their experts on Ireland and it is likely that the engraving of the ring published in the book was done by him. Ms Delamer notes that the Croker engraving was used in a book called *Finger Ring Lore* by William Jones in 1870 and labelled 'The Claddagh Ring'. Croker, being well acquainted with County Cork, which was his main collection area for folklore, may have seen Meade's rings in Kinsale; he may even have been a Friendly Brother. Whatever the precise sequence of events, by 1850 the Claddagh ring had arrived and its popularity has never been eclipsed.

By the turn of the century it was as important a part of Galway lore as the tribes. In 1906 William Dillon, a local jeweller, published an article in the *Galway Archæological and Historical Journal* called 'The "Claddagh" Ring'. The article was partly written by the editor so it is not clear who insisted on the double quotation marks around the word Claddagh as if to remind learned readers of its doubtful provenance. (By a nice coincidence the neighbouring paper, 'An Old Galway Silversmith' by Robert Day FSA, tells something of the story of Richard Joyes (Joyce), the man associated with the legend of the ring.) The article begins in something of a low-key manner:

Rings the device of which consists of two hands clasped in sign of friendship are common. And the same may be said of rings with a heart for a device. The emblematic character is pretty obvious in either case. The ring worn by the peasantry as a wedding-ring, and commonly known as the 'Claddagh' ring, has a more elaborate device, with much more character and originality. It consists, as we are all probably aware, of two hands holding between them or presenting a heart: and over the heart is a crown.

As means of comparison he describes 'a ring of base metal which Miss Redington picked up in Normandy', which has a crowned heart: ' . . . the floriated ends of the hoop may possibly be, but are not necessarily, some sort of reminiscence of the *hands* of the design.' The article is illustrated by a photograph of six *fede* rings, all of which have affinities with the Claddagh version. The first is an original Galway ring made by George Robinson, 'a goldsmith who probably came from England, and flourished in Galway early in the latter half of the 18th century.' The design is recognisable as 'Claddagh' but Dillon is careful to state that Robinson was not the original deviser of the pattern:

> . . . it is quite certain that Robinson did not invent or introduce the design, but found it already in use. It would be quite impossible to believe that the country people, so tenacious as they are of old customs and traditions, should have universally

adopted a new fashion in the 18th century, a fashion introduced into Galway by an English goldsmith. Nevertheless, the fact remains that of the hundreds worn throughout the district, there do not appear to be any of older date than the time of Robinson. Is it not reasonable to suppose that the older rings were made of base metal, perhaps, and were discarded in the 18th century and destroyed when it became a fashion, perhaps a sign of respectability, to wear gold ones only?

In spite of his assertion that many of the early Claddagh wedding rings were made in brass, bronze and silver, Dillon is impressed by the readiness of 'the local peasantry for many generations' to pay large sums of money for the 'orthodox' ring (four times the amount that was the norm in 'the Athlone district'). Galway is 'the trade centre' of Dillon's region of interest. In this area he includes the Aran Islands in the west, Connemara north through Joyce Country to Killary and the city, but east and south 'not more than 12 miles at the most'. He is insistent that in spite of the name it would be a mistake to infer that 'the use of the ring was among the peculiar customs' of the Claddagh people, though the Claddagh is 'in many respects a separate community'. He suggests that it was the universal use of the ring by Claddagh women that produced the name association. (It may have been an entrepreneurial instinct that made him anxious to associate this eminently saleable piece of jewellery with a picturesque part of his own city.)

In a poignant aside he relates a story told him by a

Galway pawnbroker, John Kirwan, that during the famine years of '46 and '47 he had left on his hands many Claddagh rings 'on which he had advanced cash ... to the extent of £500.' These were pawned by the people of the Claddagh, 'who were then emigrating in hundreds'.

> Mr Kirwan seeing no prospect of them being ever redeemed, realised his money by selling them as old gold to be broken up and consigned to the melting-pot. The 'Claddagh' ring was not at that time the fashionable ring which it is now, and there being no purchasers, these fine old rings, many of them being the rare old G. R. rings now valued for £5 each, were consigned to the melting-pot at the comparatively low price to be obtained for old gold. The fact is that the Claddagh population was at this time greatly reduced, hundreds going to the U S A, where to the present day there exists a colony of them, at Boston, called Claddagh, after their ancestral village.

Ida Delamer challenges Dillon's figures as being badly out of proportion to the population of the Claddagh of the period, but the story remains a sad little footnote to the social cataclysm that the 1840s brought.

Earlier in the article Dillon reveals that the Claddagh was the only ring ever made in Ireland for Queen Victoria, and that Edward VII wore 'one of these when passing through this portion of his dominions'. (Edward came to Ireland in 1903 on a post-coronation visit that was not universally popular; the ring is precisely the kind of gift that is given on such an occasion.) Though Dillon is too polite to say so, it was his father Thomas Dillon, then based in Waterford, that made the ring for the dear little Queen in 1849. The Delamer article also makes clear that it was the enterprise of jewellers in Galway that really created the modern ring and its popularity at home and abroad. She quotes the text of an advertisement in the *Galway Archæological and Historical Society Journal* for 1900 in which the firm of T. Dillon & Sons [one of them the William of the 1906 article] offered not only Claddagh rings but also 'Original Claddagh brooches, bangles and scarf pins'. This firm, so closely associated with the design of the ring, today maintains a small Claddagh Ring Museum in Quay Street, Galway. On display, along with memorabilia of the old city, are some of the earliest Claddagh rings in existence. Other exhibits include examples of rings at various stages of production, from wax 'blanks' to the finished product, and a selection of the tools used in their manufacture.

The Galway jewellery was usually made by the *cire perdue* or lost-wax method. The object, first modelled in wax, is coated with clay or plaster of Paris except for one vent. When the coating is hard the wax is melted out through the vent and the metal forced in to make the cast. Though most of the older rings were made from soft pure gold more modern ones use alloys to provide a price range. The heart on the bezel has tended to grow smaller and flatter and the crown wider. The popularity of the design, however modified from the original, is undiminished. As Ida Delamer notes: 'Today every Irish jeweller displays a profusion of Claddagh rings, brooches, neck pendants, bracelets, earrings, cuff links and other jewellery.'

The most effective rebuttal of the Halls' romantic story of solid gold rings being passed as heirlooms from mother to first-born daughter is the fact that, as Ida Delamer reveals, 'all extant Claddagh rings made prior to 1840 are male rings'. This she neatly establishes by measuring the internal diameters and finding that they are more than 1.9 cm, the standard lower measure for male rings. She makes the point that even if these were originally owned by Claddagh *men* it was unlikely that working fishermen would have worn a ring with as large a bezel as a Claddagh. They may, however, have been kept 'for good' and worn only on occasions like the St John's Day processions. Where surviving rings have inscriptions these are done in English and not the Gaelic of the Claddagh. (One described by Dillon has a posy, 'Yours in Hart'.) As to their being made in gold, she feels that such would have been beyond the means of the Claddagh people. The Dillon article mentions that one of the 'Claddagh' rings shown in his photograph is bronze, made from an old coin, and probably 'made from the coin in the same way that sailors often make rings from silver coins, on a marline spike'. Kurt Ticher in an article entitled 'The Claddagh Ring: A West of Ireland Folklore Custom' (*The Antique Dealer and Collectors Guide*, August 1980) comments upon the carat-rating of the Claddagh rings in the Honorable Garech Browne's collection in the National Museum of Ireland:

Until the Garech Browne collection was assayed it was assumed as a matter of course that the Claddagh rings were 'solid gold'. Until 1784 that term meant 22 carat, later 18 carat . . . It was something of a shock to discover that not only the rings in the Garech Brown collection but also others examined for fineness varied from 18 carat at most down to 7 carat or even 6 . . .

I can only suggest one reason for the variation in fineness. Because rings were not sent for hall-marking to Dublin, it was not necessary for the Galway makers to comply with the regulations. The poor fishermen of the Claddagh made what was for them a great sacrifice to obtain their rings, telling the goldsmiths how much they could afford to pay. They in turn would have fixed the caratage to bring the ring within the customer's means. In the end, to a proud people to whom £3 was a virtual fortune, poverty dictated the fineness of the gold.

Perhaps the Halls' use of the word 'solid' was a little bit enthusiastic and all that glisters might have passed for the real thing. Dillon tells us that Andrew Robinson, an early artificer who worked in Galway around 1800, used to make the rings from guinea-gold, using the actual coins as his material. One answer to Ms Delamer's objections may be that the surviving rings upon which she bases her conclusions were originally commissioned and owned by wealthy people. Such a provenance might well explain their survival.

The origin of the design remains obscure; it may have come about by some kind of evolutionary process gradually incorporating 'gemmel' and other elements. The rings made by the contemporaries Richard Joyce of Galway and Thomas Meade of Kinsale show sufficient similarity to each other to suggest that they used an already existing design or variation of such. Kurt Ticher in the article mentioned earlier can find no connection between the two men, who apparently worked independently. He does establish, however, that interest in the design seems to have lapsed when Joyce stopped his working career about 1730, and it was not revived until George Robinson began professional manufacture some time after 1784 when his name was registered in Goldsmiths' Hall in Dublin. The gaps in the ring's history and its general air of romance have caused myth and folklore to fill the historical gap.

5

MARGARET OF THE BRIDGES
AND RICHARD OF ALGIERS

Not inappropriately the name of one of the tribes of the 'citie' figures in both the myth and the discoverable facts about the origin of the Claddagh ring. The first is a story of wonder associated with the sixteenth-century Margaret Joyce, the second nearly as unlikely-sounding but probably true. Hardiman recounts Margaret's story in his history and the Rev Cæsar Otway (1780–1842), the Protestant activist who joined William Carleton to his merry band of anti-Catholic scribes, gives a typically colourful account of the tale in *A Tour in Connaught* (1839). Even the walking Frenchman Le Chevalier de la Tocnaye whose account of a tour of Ireland at the end of the eighteenth century was published as *Promenade d'un français dans l'Irlande* in 1797 mentions the bridge-builder.

It is said also that thirteen families, whose names are still common, laid the city's foundations, and tradition avers that, while a good lady of the name of Joyce watched the masons who built Galway

Bridge at her expense, an eagle dropped a chain of gold in her lap, and placed a crown on her head. The gold chain is still preserved by the Joyce family – according to the story told to me. The people have always loved fables – had Galway become a Rome this one would certainly have been believed.

According to Otway she was the daughter of John Joyce and met her first husband, Don Domingo de Rona, as she was washing her linen in the Galway river ('the broad transparent stream which runs out of Lough Corrib'). He was a wine merchant from La Coruña in northwest Spain (the 'Corrunna' where 'slowly and sadly' Sir John Moore was laid down) and a regular visitor to Galway, which was then famous for its wines. They were married and went to live in Spain. Otway suggests that the husband was much older: ' . . . not long after he died (as old cavaliers are apt to who marry late) and Donna De Rona came home a sparkling and wealthy widow.'

Hardiman's account is told in much more sober language.

Upon his decease, having no issue by him, she married Oliver Oge Ffrench, who was Mayor of Galway in 1596. So far the narrative is probable and consistent, but what follows will try the credulity of the reader. It relates that this lady, during the absence of her second husband, on a voyage, erected most part of the bridges of the Province of Connaught, at her own expense! And that she was one day sitting before the workmen, when an eagle, flying over her head, let fall into her bosom, a gold ring crowned with a brilliant stone, the nature of which no lapidary could ever discover. It was preserved by her descendants, as a most valuable relique in 1661 (the date of the MS from which this account is taken) as a mark supposed to have been sent from Heaven of its approbation of her good works and charity.

Hely Dutton has a slight variation of the story which he appends to the name of Margaret's husband in the list of city mayors in his *Survey* (1824):

> While the mayor her husband was at sea she built the bridges of Connaught at her own expense. One day reviewing the workmen, an eagle flying over her head let fall a stone ring.

The coat of arms of the Joyce family shows 'argent an eagle with two heads displayed gules' but since the grant of the coat of arms may have been made before the coming of the air-mailed ring the appositeness of the decoration is probably coincidental.

Margaret Fitzjohn Joyce Ffrench remains an elusive character, known historically for her pontifical preoccupations and in some way as the recipient of the heavenly origin of the ring of Claddagh. The story has all the elements of traditional myth; the girl discovered at her laundry by her future husband is a recurring motif in European fairytales, and eagles are notorious for dropping things. Aeschylus (525–456 BC) the father of Greek tragedy was killed, according to the traditional story, by a tortoise dropped by an eagle on his bald head (in mistake for a stone). The 'brilliant stone' which landed in Margaret's lap and which no lapidary could identify may have some connection with the belief in *aetites,* precious stones with magical or medicinal properties that were according to legend to be found in eagles' nests.

The only date that we can accurately assign to Margaret na Drehide, as she is surnamed in Hardiman's account, is that her husband was Mayor of Galway in 1596-7, but the family legend was jealously preserved by the tribe. As Ida Delamer notes in an appendix to her definitive article, the Blake family papers contain the note:

A curious relic has been preserved in the senior line of the Joyces of Joyce Country for 300 years; it is a stone of the shape and size of an egg and of polished surface, possibly a species of crystal. According to the tradition of the family the stone was dropped by an eagle into the lap of Margaret, daughter of John Joyce and wife of Oliver Oge Ffrench who was mayor of Galway 1596-1597. The relic is the possession of Martin B Joyce formally of Tinahille in Joyce Country by now, 1905, residing in the town of Galway.

The story of Richard Joyce or Joyes, as he preferred to spell it, begins in 1679. A native of Galway, he was then on his way to the West Indies and was captured by an Algerian pirate and purchased as a slave by a wealthy Turkish goldsmith who taught him his trade. The story appears as a footnote to page 15 of Hardiman and is quoted in full in the paper, 'An Old Galway Silversmith' by Robert Day:

Several individuals of this name have long felt grateful to the memory of William III from the following circumstance. On the accession of that monarch to the throne of England, one of the first acts of his reign was to send an ambassador to Algiers, to demand the immediate release of all the British subjects detained there in slavery. The Dey and Council, intimidated, reluctantly complied with this demand. Among those released was a young man of the name of Joyes, a native of Galway, who, fourteen years before, was captured on his passage to the West Indies by an Algerine corsair. On his arrival at Algiers, he was purchased by a wealthy Turk, who followed the profession of a goldsmith, and who observing his slave, Joyes, to be tractable and ingenious, instructed him in his trade, in which he speedily became an adept. The Moor, as soon as he heard of his release, offered him, in case he should remain, his only daughter in marriage, and with her half his property; but all these, with other tempting and advantageous proposals, Joyes resolutely declined. On his return to Galway he married and followed the business of goldsmith with considerable success, and having acquired a handsome independence, he was enabled to purchase the estate of Rahoon (which lies about two miles west of the town), from Colonel Whaley, one of Cromwell's old officers. Joyes, having no son, bequeathed his property to his three daughters, two of whom only were married, one to Andrew Roe French of Rahoon, ancestor to the late Andrew French of Rahoon, to whom in addition to their own, the unmarried daughter left her third; the second daughter was married to the ancestor of the late Martin Lynch, a banker, who in her right inherited the remainder of the estate. Some of Joyes' silver work stamped with his mark and the initial letters of his name, are still remaining.

The mark is the anchor which as a town sign is shared with many other places, including Birmingham, where, according to Dillon's article, imitation Claddagh rings were to be found on sale. He also suggests that the Munster rings, one of which appears in his photograph, may very well be Brummagem imports. The other appropriate town mark was the ship which often appeared alongside the anchor on pieces of Galway workmanship. In separating the facts from the Scheherezade story of the slave who made good and was offered his master's daughter, such unimpeachable evidence of Joyce's ability and certain location in Galway is reassuring. There is no doubt that his punch mark is on the 'Claddagh' ring in the Garech Browne collection and dated 1700. His design has all the elements that we associate with the nineteenth-century ring and differs from earlier *fede* rings in that he has crowned the clasped heart. Kurt Ticher suggests in the article mentioned earlier that Joyce 'may have got the inspiration for the design while working for the goldsmith in Algiers' but that there is no evidence for it. He goes on to say, 'There are rings which resemble the Claddagh ring, but they deviate in detail, and do not include a crown. Why would Joyce have added one to an emblem of hands and heart?' Why indeed! If he in fact did originate the design we know, it may be that the crown was added as a token of loyalty to the reigning monarch, perhaps Queen Anne who came to the throne in 1702. This would have been an astute move for an ambitious businessman of his time and city to make. He may even have crowned the heart as a tribute to William III, who had him delivered from his captivity.

The awkward problem of the Meade rings remains. They are contemporaneous with the extant Joyce ring and have no discoverable connection with Galway or the Claddagh. However, the fact that experts like Kurt Ticher can find nothing to link Joyce and Meade does not mean that they were unknown to each other. Certainly the similarity of their designs is remarkable and there are no rings in existence that can be assigned to any year after 1700 and before the 1780s. If Dillon is right in his assertion that when George Robinson began to renew the manufacture of Galway rings in 1784 he used an already existing design, we are left with two possibilities: one, that Joyce's design on rings made up till his retirement in the 1730s was remembered and commissioned from Robinson by richer clients; or two, that Joyce's design had been copied by amateur ringsmiths on bezels of guinea-gold or even bronze and so preserved. Either way the name of Richard Joyce, miraculously delivered from heathen captivity, is with justice or not, forever associated with a ring whose striking design is nowadays unexceptionably interpreted as: 'This is my heart which I give to you crowned with my love.'

One of the rings illustrated in Dillon's photograph is slightly different from the rest. The bezel is done in *opus interrasile* (fretwork); the parts of the band that hold the centre of the bezel could be hands but might simply be a non-specific engraved design. The 'heart' section is rather triangular than heart-shaped and the 'crown' might well be five small hemispheres set on top. It looks like a Claddagh ring at a different stage of evolution. According to Dillon it was procured in Brittany in the 1870s. He notes (and we can sense his professional approbation):

And we have heard that in Brittany, just as here in the West of Ireland, these rings, used as wedding-rings, are highly prized and are handed down as heirlooms, while a new ring is procured for every fresh marriage, the ring inherited or used earlier never doing duty again.

He dismisses regretfully any suggestion that the similarity of the rings and that of the temperament, occupation and geographical configuration of the habitats of the Celtic inhabitants suggests a remote antiquity for the design:

We must rather conclude that it was chance that brought to both people the same design (through intercourse with Spain, perhaps, but we do not know); and that it was a similar poetic temperament – for we know that they do resemble each other in temperament – that led both peoples to appreciate the charm and appropriateness of the design, and to adopt it as their own.

Ticher casts doubt on any Hispanic connection: 'Dillon's ascription to Brittany or Spain cannot be verified: the writer's approach to three museums in Spain, and to Malta, proved negative.'

A last word about the design may as well be heard from a professional engraver. Robert Gibbings (1889–1958), the Cork-born designer whose engaging travel books were decorated by his own exquisite engravings, visited Galway for his book *Lovely is the Lee* (1945). Speaking of Claddagh rings he notes professionally that:

Although the device of two hands clasping a heart is not uncommon in many parts of Europe, the same with the crown added is extremely rare. It has however its counterpart in Spain, whence the design may have been brought to Galway by early traders.

Like the better known posy rings, an occasional one of those of Claddagh design had a motto inscribed on its inner surface. But a simple thought like 'Yours in hart,' such as we may find in Galway, scarcely compares with the more elaborate sentiments often found in the 'posies'. Nowhere in the west are we likely to come across such sophistication as: 'Love him who gave thee this ring of gold,/ 'Tis he must kiss thee when thou'rt old,' or a line that offers such food for conjecture as: 'Feare God, and lye abed till noone,' or ambition like that of the

bishop who, at his fourth wedding had inscribed:
'If I survive I'll make thee five.'

6
—

LOVE AND FRIENDSHIP

As William Dillon implies in his 1906 article, it is pointless to claim antiquity for the design of the Claddagh ring and this is the most likely explanation for there not being very much lore. The ring seems to have played no discoverable part in nineteenth-century romances nor does it figure in any of the folktales. Perhaps the nineteenth-century jewellers who developed the design commercially and established the ring's popularity missed a trick in not generating a mythology. The story of Margaret Joyce's eagle and Richard Joyce's escape from the Casbah are romantic enough, but there is not much else. The motto 'Let love and friendship reign' does fit well with the elements of the Claddagh design and the heart symbolising love, the hand faith in friendship and the crown loyalty, complete the mood.

There is a tradition that the ring may be worn in three different ways, each with a special significance. When placed on the right hand with the heart facing out it indicates that the wearer has not yet found a lover; when worn on the right hand with the heart facing in it may mean that someone has taken an option; and when worn on the left hand it means that love is plighted. The rings have become increasingly popular as wedding-bands, and not just in Ireland. Ideally they should have been received as a gift from a friend or a lover, and if worn after such a presentation with the heart pointing out it may be a sign that love has died or that the object of affection is no longer present.

These significant positions are all the lore that can be ascribed to the ring. Real folklore, I suppose, requires a slow growth from antiquity, and popular as the ring became, its origin was too recent to generate a Deirdre or a Gráinne. There is very little native Irish writing about the ring, the best known being Patrick B. Kelly's ballad which is reproduced in this book.

Whatever its origins, the ring, with its loving hands, its beating heart and its sovereign diadem is a talisman of love and friendship, a desideratum in a country that is still in parts distressful. It is an honourable part of the story of Ireland's western capital and may well be the last relic of a fascinating piece of Irish social history. There is no longer a Claddagh for the moon to rise over, as in the 1940s' song, but the ring remains as its memorial, and a great-hearted, crowning one it is.

BIBLIOGRAPHY

Annála Ríoghachta Éireann (1632-6) (*Annals of the Kingdom of Ireland by the Four Masters*, trans. John O'Donovan). Dublin, 1841-51.

Augustinian Fathers (eds.). *The Gailliv.* Galway, 1901.

Automobile Association. *Illustrated Roadbook of Ireland.* Dublin, 1966.

Day, Robert. 'An Old Galway Silversmith', in *Cork Historical & Archæological Society Journal*, X. Cork, 1904.

De La Tocnaye, Chev. *Promenade d'un Français dans l'Irlande 1796-7* (*A Frenchman's Walk through Ireland*). Cork, 1798; reprinted Belfast, 1984.

Delamer, Ida. 'The Claddagh Ring', in *Irish Arts Review Yearbook*, XII, 1996.

Dillon, William. 'The "Claddagh" Ring', in *Galway Archæological Society Journal*, IV, 1905-6.

Dutton, Hely. *A Statistical and Agricultural Survey of the County of Galway.* Dublin, 1824.

Gibbings, Robert. *Lovely Is the the Lee.* London, 1945.

Gwynn, Stephen. *A Holiday in Connemara.* London, 1908.

———— . *The Famous Cities of Ireland.* Dublin, 1915.

Hall, A. M. & S. C. *Ireland, Its Scenery, Character, &c.* London, 1842.

———— . *Hand-Books for Ireland: The West and Connamara.* London, 1853.

Hardiman, James. *The History of the Town & County of Galway.* Galway, 1820.

Hayward, Richard. *This Is Ireland. Connacht and the City of Galway.* London, 1952.

Inglis, Henry D. *Ireland in 1834,* II. London, 1835.

Joyce, Cecily. *Claddagh Ring Story.* Galway, 1990.

Killanin, Lord and Michael V. Duignan.*The Shell Guide to Ireland.* (rev. Peter Harbison). Dublin, 1989.

Lewis, Samuel. *A Topographical Dictionary of Ireland* Dublin, 1837.

Lynd, Robert. *Rambles in Ireland.* London, 1912.

Mac Lochlainn, Alf. 'The Claddagh Piscatorial School', in *Two Galway Schools.* Galway, 1993.

Morton, Henry Vollam. *In Search of Ireland.* London,1930.

O'Dowd, Peadar. *Down by the Claddagh.* Galway, 1993.

Ó Cearbhaill, D. (ed.). *Galway: Town and Gown.* Galway, 1984.

O'Flaherty, Roderick. *Chorographic Description of West or h-Iar Connaught. 1684.* (ed. James Hardiman). Dublin, 1846.

Sullivan, M. D. *Old Galway.* Cambridge, 1942.

Otway, Cæsar. *A Tour in Connaught.* Dublin, 1939.

Rynne, Etienne. *Tourist Trail of Old Galway.* Galway, 1977.

Thackeray, William M. *The Irish Sketchbook.* London, 1843.

Ticher, Kurt. 'The Claddagh Ring: A West of Ireland Folklore Custom', in *The Antique Dealer and Collectors Guide.* August 1980.

Young, Arthur. *A Tour of Ireland (1776-1778).* London, 1780.

Wilde, William. *Lough Corrib, Its Shores and Islands.* Dublin, 1872.

Photograph courtesy of the National Museum of Ireland